THE CON...

Apply fo... ...

On-Your-Own

In Just Four (4) Months Receive Your Social Security Disability Insurance Benefits!

J.D. Davis

DavisPublishing.Org

Pasadena, CA

The Concise Guide to Apply for Disability On-Your-Own
In Just Four (4) Months Receive Your Social Security
Disability Insurance Benefits!
By: J.D. Davis
All Rights Reserved. Copyright © 2016 by Jarita D. Davis

Published by: Jarita D. Davis
DavisPublishing.Org
Pasadena, CA 91105
First printing October 2016
ISBN: 978-0-9863876-1-6

To God be the Glory!

Dedication

TONY L. DAVIS,
My Beloved Husband, Best Friend, Partner and Sweetest Caregiver

And for the Memory of
My Mommy, Daddy, and Sissy
*For always encouraging me to pursue my dreams and passion, and to
"Always put God first."*

To my loving brother and his beautiful wife, my sister-in-law,
John and Janet

To my brother-in-law, Gary *who showed me loyalty and
encouragement to write this second book.*

And, to "Family and Friends" *who were loving and supported us
during our temporary season of change and trials.*

TABLE OF CONTENTS

INTRODUCTION

The **Concise Guide to Apply for Disability On-Your-Own** was written to shorten the content of the original publication of "Apply for Disability On-Your-Own" (**AFDOYO**). This **Concise Guide** explains how to successfully **"apply and quickly receive"** your **Social Security Disability Insurance benefits**, and to give an update in laymen's terms on any essential updates since the original AFDOYO book's publication.

The Concise Guide is a shortened version of AFDOYO and explains how to **EASILY** apply for SSDI. It also shares updated **"easy-read"** information and covers essential sections of Part One and most of Part Two, from the original AFDOYO book.

As mentioned in the original AFDOYO book's Prologue, please know these books were **written to help you** by sharing my experience of successfully applying for Social Security Disability Insurance, and **within four (4) months receiving my SSDI benefits** – and being approved the very **first time without hiring** an attorney and/or advocate.

Be at peace and receive **ALL** of your **SSDI benefits**, while not being able to work due to your disability. You paid FICA taxes for your Social Security Disability Insurance, which is no different than paying for regular insurance – **when in need – use it. SSDI** is not a handout from the government, remember **you** paid into it!

www.applyfordisability-oyo.com

1

PROLOGUE

Ladies and Gentlemen, here it is. If you are looking for a book that will help you with understanding Social Security Disability Insurance and how to **"quickly receive"** your **benefits** without going through attorneys or advocates and to receive your benefits **"on-your-own"** in **just four (4) months, <u>please read on</u>.**

You are about to join me on a passage through an experience of learning the process of becoming officially disabled and the need of emotional, spiritual, and financial support. Please know I am writing this book to help you – in sharing my personal story of successfully applying for **Social Security Disability Insurance (SSDI)**, and, I was **APPROVED** the **<u>"FIRST TIME APPLYING"</u>** on my own with **<u>NO</u>** **assistance** from an attorney, advocate, referrals, and **<u>NO</u>** appeals, **<u>NO</u>** courtrooms, **<u>NO</u>** judges, etc., and **received my SSDI benefits <u>within four (4) months</u>!**

If you require a family member or friend to take care of your personal financial business, you may want to share this book with them to assist you in applying for your Social Security Disability Insurance benefits.

If you are mentally and/or physically dependent and have no one but yourself, then I recommend hiring an attorney and/or advocate to help you, and to read Part One of the original "Apply for Disability On-Your-Own" book which may help you with **learning more about yourself** being disabled, and to help give you **faith, hope and strength** to keep moving forward in a positive manner during this time of your life.

IMPORTANT NOTE: The Social Security Administration covers disability benefit payments through two separate programs. This book covers the "Social Security Disability Insurance" program **ONLY** with proof of receiving timely benefits. This book does **NOT** include and/or cover the government assistance Supplemental Security Income (SSI) disability program's process.

So, let's get started with our journey. "Hello. My name is J.D. and I just had an appointment with my neurologist and learned that I would not be able to work my normal career path, and that I am now disabled." I've worked since being 15 years old, graduated from high school, went to college, acquired two degrees (i.e., BA, MS) and worked over 35+

career consistent years. I was blessed to have two wonderful parents who wholeheartedly supported my vision and dreams, had a progressive and lucrative career, and married a wonderfully, hard-working and very caring and supportive entrepreneur. The two of us together have helped others, and had started to prepare for our retirement years. I have a beautiful step-daughter, and adorable grand-daughter who was born on my birthday.

Life was going well, until I received the news from my neurologist -- that traveling, intense work, etc., and my fast paced career life would need to slow down tremendously due to an old brain injury. Ugh. Lord, help me.

Since 1979, I had always planned that if an incident of **"disability"** was ever to occur while working we would be prepared for it and therefore, always paid additional disability insurance through my employer. As many Americans caught in the middle of transition due to being disabled, etc., we were now placed in that situation with my career -- and with that said, **"NO Disability benefits"** were available through an employer or anyone else.

This was a very huge eye opening experience of both *"learning and blessings"* which I decided to share with others in this book. The first part of the book will help you in learning about yourself, faith, hope, and what is available if you ever find yourself being disabled. Also, it will help you learn how to adapt from the perspective of a person who became surprisingly disabled, and was successfully able to receive benefits from Social Security Disability by applying on their own with **no assistance from an attorney and/or advocate.**

The second part of this book will disclose how to successfully apply and **QUICKLY** receive your **"Notice of Award"** in order to receive your SSDI benefits and start a new chapter of your life.

This book is written for you, if you are disabled, need financial support, and want to receive your Social Security Disability Insurance (SSDI) benefits in a short period of time versus becoming part of the horror stories of waiting for a year or more. Also, if you want to keep all of your hard earned benefits, versus having attorneys and/or advocates take a portion, when you **CAN DO** the application on your own, but was afraid to ask for assistance. This book will assist you in how to move through the application process, build confidence, and receive your benefits in a timely manner. This book is not a technical book, it was written to be easily understood by applicants to apply for disability benefits, and receive their benefit award within four (4) months – on their own.

This book was not written for people to abuse the SSDI system to just use as a secondary welfare system which has been a subject in the media. This book is not to be used for fraud or waste of the SSDI system.

It is a book to help people who are truly disabled, not capable of working and who need their Social Security Disability Insurance benefits in order to live life with purpose and to help them rest, be restored, increase faith, and heal emotionally and physically.

So, you may ask, "What led you to write this 'self-help disability' book?" To start, my natural self and passion is to help people of all colors and all walks of life. I personally know people from various socio-economic backgrounds, for example: individuals who are regular working people, upper class, middle class, underserved, homeless, millionaires and billionaires; and religions i.e., Christians, Jewish, Muslim, new age, and non-religious individuals, etc. and believe me everyone has issues. People are all different in beliefs, life experiences and action, but everyone lives through "good" days and "rough" days. How people handle their life is an individual decision, and should be unconditionally respected.

Personally, I learned from my first job in 1973 to today, that my "purpose and work life" is very important to me. My parents would always remind me to put God first in my life; they injected the importance of strong work ethics, family and to play later. With that said, the priority of growing into adulthood – was and is to stay focused as a believer and follower of Jesus Christ, have a successful career and purpose to help others, family commitment, etc. and that is what I believe.

QUICK SUMMARY OF READING THIS BOOK:

Over the next few chapters of this book, you will discover how to "quickly" receive Social Security Disability Insurance (SSDI) benefits by applying on-your-own via the Social Security website, AND receive your SSDI benefits in a few months as follows:

- Knowing the importance of **"Faith and Hope"** during this time, and accepting the "Disability" Decision,

- Understanding Social Security Disability Insurance and other options,

- Can you **"Do It Yourself,"** so that you can keep **ALL** of your hard-earned money, versus hire an attorney/advocate,

- Learn the **"Success Points"** in how to successfully apply on-your-own and receive benefits the first time submitted,

- In just **Four (4) Months** Receive Social Security Disability Benefits by doing it on your own, and

- The Beginning of a **"New Life" Chapter!**

*"The fear of the LORD is the instruction of wisdom,
And before honor is humility."*
–Proverbs 15:33 NKJV

PART ONE

FAITH AND HOPE

Are you wondering what is going to happen now that you're aware that you will not be able to work – and have been told you are **disabled**? Or, are you planning to help a family member or friend apply for Social Security Disability Insurance? **I know the feeling**. This is not a popular, sexy, or glamourous subject period.

"Disability" is a subject some people just – **do not want to discuss, understand, talk about, say "The D-word,"** or **even think about**. It is **surreal. Lonely. Unbelievable. Hurtful. Very scary.** But, there is an answer to help you through this season. That's right. This is just a season, that will pass in time. Believe me, it will pass. Let me help you with a portion of my humbling story of **faith and hope**.

Here we go…it's been **22 days** of no writing. **OH NO!** I thought it was only **TWO (2) DAYS** of not writing this book, but, I need to date my writing days and counted **22**

days! My days have been rough, memory issues, head pains, and foggy. Reality has set in. Had multiple brain surgeries…but, I must continue and what better chapter to start this book and help in getting us through this season than, **"Faith and Hope."**

During this time of life in making the "disability decision," the reality of it all truly sets in – and you have to release all of your doubts, fears, and anxiety. As mentioned in the Prologue, every day is a good day, and some days will be rough. *(NOTE: I do not believe in "bad" days, therefore, you will read in the book as it relates to "days", the replacement of "bad with rough.")*

While applying and waiting for your SSDI approval or any decision at this time, you can take on a **very anxious state of mind. But taking one day at a time is highly recommended.** Do not think of tomorrow, just get through today and you will be just fine. It's good to plan and have short and long term goals, but, when your health is being compromised it is mentally safer to relax and take one day at a time, and put all long-term goals to the side until your health is stable.

With that said, during the Disability application timeframe the main focus is to concentrate on your doctor's guidance and your SSDI application process. We'll talk more about specific details in Part Two.

This sub-chapter is short, but extremely important – remember to have and keep **"<u>Faith and Hope</u>."** Believe you can do it, and all will be well for you emotionally, spiritually, and physically. Your mind, body, and soul will relax and be open to complete your SSDI application process with less anxiety and a **"can-do"** manner of approaching your goal and the end-result – **your** **Social Security Disability Notice of Award!**

MAKING THE "DISABILITY" DECISION

So – let's get started on **"Making the 'Disability' Decision."** First of all, what is the meaning of "disability?" Or, should I ask, "What does this 'disability' terminology mean, since that is what I am now being classified, at this moment?"

I might sound a little perturbed about this subject, because it was all new to me, and I did not expect to deal with "disability" in life. But, I am realistic that "things happen to

11

all people," and I am very thankful to God for my faith and hope of this being a temporary season, coupled with a new life of learning, blessings, purpose, and a sphere of influence that will hopefully help many people in our nation and around the world to ex-pats, who are going through the same situation or condition.

The American Heritage Dictionary of the English Language, 4th Edition, defines: "disability – 1a. The condition of being disabled; incapacity. b. The period of such a condition: *never received a penny during her disability.* 2. A disadvantage or deficiency, especially a physical or mental impairment that interferes with or prevents normal achievement in a particular area. 3. Something that hinders or incapacitates. 4. A legal incapacity or disqualification."

After reading the definition of "disability" from the dictionary, it brought me to tears. That is not me! I am fine. I am not that person. Well, the definition brings light in learning who I have become during this period of life of being classified as "disabled."

Okay – STOP! Yes, this is real, and I just had a quick "pity party" for myself. It is normal to have a "quick" pity party, and it is **wise to release your pity and move on with faith and hope** for your future.

Now with that said, it is time to move on to claim and make an affirmation that the "self-pity parties" are OVER. **Dear Reader, you will not experience another pity-party in this book,** because it is now time to **take control and take action,** so that you can prepare to move into your new stage of life by accepting and embracing your disability season, coupled with finding means to help rest, restore, renew, heal and survive physically, emotionally and financially. To that end and continuing to move forward, let's get to work!

Prepare for Success

Your next step is to *"prepare for success"* in order to complete the SSDI application process, and receive your SSDI Notice of Award in just four (4) months. **Preparation will entail becoming comfortable with your subject** by learning more about the purpose of The Social Security Administration, Social Security Disability Insurance, alternative options, answering preparedness questions and studying Part Two of this book, as it relates to achieving your mission by **receiving your Social Security Disability Insurance benefits in a timely manner.**

WHAT IS SOCIAL SECURITY DISABILITY INSURANCE?

In order to proceed successfully with the Social Security Disability Insurance **(SSDI)** application process, it is important to actually understand, **"What is SSDI?"**

 The Social Security Administration (SSA) website, which is: "www.socialsecurity.gov" section on history greatly explains the origin of Social Security, Social Security Disability, Medicare, and I recommend you visit the website to learn of the origin and purpose of Social Security and SSDI. Please note: it is not necessary at this time to review it, but for general knowledge it is a nice read and gives an appropriate awareness to the subject.

For example, per the Social Security Bulletin, Volume 60, 1997, Number 2, states: *"Disability benefits under Title II of the Social Security Act became part of the law in 1956, and Medicare came into being in 1965. We might assume, therefore, that the first cash disability payments made by the Social Security Administration (SSA) occurred sometime around 1956, and the first medical benefit claims would have been processed sometime around 1965."* With that said, there are numerous Reports & Studies researched and published on the www.socialsecurity.gov/history website and the data is very interesting as it relates to how long the program(s) have been in existence and original purpose(s).

But, for a quick reference and real understanding of SSDI and "Disability Benefits," the best answer to the question of, "What is SSDI?" can be found on the www.socialsecurity.gov website in the Social Security Administration (SSA) Publication No. 05-10029, ICN 456000, page 4, as follows: *"Disability is something most people do not like to think about. But the chances that you will become disabled probably are greater than you realize. Studies show that a 20-year-old worker has a 1-in-4 chance of becoming disabled before reaching full retirement age...We pay disability benefits through two programs: the Social Security disability insurance program and the Supplemental Security Income (SSI) program."*

NOTE: this book and the SSA Publication No. 05-10029 covers **ONLY** the Social Security disability insurance program. If you need information on the Supplemental Security Income (SSI) program, please visit the website (www.ssa.gov/disabilityssi/ssi.html) and review the publications for the SSI program.

The aforementioned quote from the SSA Publication says it all. It is so true, many of us do not expect our bodies to become disabled, but, sometimes they do – and we should make all attempts to be prepared if it does by chance occur in our lifetime. Again, this is a quick reference to assist you in understanding the Social Security Disability Insurance program.

The next quote from the SSA Publication also on page 4, briefly describes the program exceptionally well, as follows: *"Social Security pays benefits to people who cannot work because they have a medical condition that is expected to last at least one year or result in death. Federal law requires this very strict definition of disability. While some programs give money to people with partial disability or short-term disability. Social Security does not."*

With that said, the above quote is a solid segue to our next sub-chapter, **"Is it True?"**

Is It True?

Please believe me, this "disability" journey is up and down, and it is imperative you attempt to stay focused, be at peace, and know yourself. To that end, in order to proceed successfully with an expeditious SSDI application process, it is extremely necessary to **"deeply"** understand and accept your current situation, and internally answer the following question about your disability, and that is, **"Is it true?"** If your doctor or medical practitioner has advised you that working full-time/part-time is not for your best interest, or that you should not work due to your medical condition; or your family has given an intervention that you listen to your physician and not work – the answer to, **"Is it true?"** is, **"Yes. It is true."**

If you have worked for many years, it is so very hard to accept the fact that you are being told **"...you are disabled."** **It's hard. But, now it is time to face it – and take a quiet moment to meditate, pray, and ponder the moment**, and then verbally say, **"Yes. It is true."** and move on with the realization, and then proceed with **reviewing all of your disability benefit options.** But, believe me. It will take time *(maybe years)*, to accept the fact that **it is true**.

Alternate Disability Options

If you are an employed individual and have **"disability insurance"** as part of your health and employment benefits – **awesome!** Now is the time to advise your employer of your situation and apply for your employer's disability benefits, if available. Some employers offer disability insurance as a benefit. The employer's disability benefit insurance is different from the government's Family and Medical Leave Act (FMLA) program. The disability insurance benefits from employers are usually between 60-80% of your salary or pay.

Disability Insurance is a "retirement investment" protection plan. You may **<u>NOT</u>** have to use your **401K or savings,** if you acquire Disability Insurance, and that includes **applying for your Social Security Disability Insurance (SSDI)! READ ON.**

NOTE: Every company is different, therefore, please verify your company's disability program for your position with your Human Resources department. You could have the option to accept that amount and conserve other disability monies regarding the difference. If you are unemployed or employed, you may have an option to apply for temporary

State disability, if your state offers it and this could help supplement your income and/or the difference of your wages. Additionally, many insurance companies have disability programs that are offered, and you may want to review those avenues.

If you are reading this book for the purpose to **"quickly" apply for SSDI,** obtaining disability benefits from an insurance company could be a research option for later, not now.

But, if you are in the research mode to **protect your retirement investment,** now is the time to review insurance companies for their **Disability Insurance Programs**. Not to promote any company, but, one that stands out is the cute, little white duck on television commercials – is one option, and the company name starts with an "A." Also, check with your auto, home…insurance company or Google "Disability Insurance" for other company options. There are many program options available, and securing **"Disability Insurance"** can help save your retirement investment, quality of life, and peace of mind. Becoming disabled and needing support is a major life event. Be prepared.

If your disability is assumed to be longer than a year, now is the time to apply for **Social Security Disability Insurance (SSDI)** which is available for the rest of your life, if your disability remains. Please note, there are periodic medical reviews based on your specific claim. The medical reviews are performed by hired SSDI medical professionals over a period of years, to re-evaluate your disability case.

To summarize the alternate disability options to research, are as follows:

1.) Employer short-term disability program
2.) Employer long-term disability program
3.) State disability program
4.) Insurance companies
5.) Social Security Disability Insurance (SSDI)

Remember to always check with your Financial/Tax professional regarding your specific situation. Now, let's move onto making the "major" decision of who should administer your SSDI application process, **"you or an attorney/advocate?"**

The Process Decision – "Them or Me?"

We have discussed making the Disability Decision, Faith and Hope, Prepare for Success, the meaning of Social Security Disability Insurance, and Alternate Disability Options. The last **"Alternate Disability Option"** briefly covered in the last subchapter was, **"Social Security Disability Insurance (SSDI)."**

Personally, after learning about my inability to work a full time career, and not having the other disability benefit options available, I had to research the **Social Security Disability Insurance (SSDI)** program.

I found out that after working for over 35 years, the FICA tax that was taken out from my paychecks since I was 15 years old, **could help support me** during this time frame in my life. **Wow! SSDI is available for individuals who have worked, paid FICA tax and need financial support to help with everyday needs.** We had planned for retirement, but, with me being disabled and my husband being my caregiver (since we did not live near family), we had to expeditiously focus on making the decision to apply, in order to help maintain our standard of living.

We heard interesting and horror stories of **how long it takes** to receive **SSDI – if approved!** All we were hearing is that it may take years to receive your SSDI Notice of Award, but, you would receive a "back payment" lump sum for your wait. Social Security Disability Insurance benefits are paid for the sixth full month after the date your disability started, and monthly benefits are based on an individual's average lifetime salary or wages.

We were hearing it could take 2-5 years and to use an attorney or advocate. We heard using an attorney/advocate would help relieve stress, in not having to worry about filling out loads of paperwork.

It was also mentioned to let the attorney/advocate just perform the application processing, because they would be able to push the paperwork through the system while you rest, but, the timing of receiving your benefits could be a long waiting process. Sounds good to have it done by a professional and to not worry about paperwork, but, the waiting period and not having control during this critical time was not a "feel good for me," but more of a *"stressor"* to the overall situation.

What a decision to make. After working in a corporate "operational" environment from manager to vice president levels, **I felt there had to be a way to bridge it all together** and for the system to work in my favor. **If I could work through the application process "on my own" with success, I <u>made a promise to publicly share my story to assist others</u>.** I strongly believed it could be done, and set a goal to receive my disability benefits **within four (4) months.**

Happily – the strategic process was successful and <u>within four (4) months</u>, I <u>received my Social Security Disability Notice of Award</u>. I'm **<u>humbled and honored</u> to share this information with all of you,** and wishing you the **<u>best</u> in your decision making.** Everyone's situation is different, and some of you may need to hire an attorney/advocate – and it is wonderful they are available to help those in need of their services. If you need an attorney/advocate to help you, I recommend you go on the Internet to find a disability attorney/advocate listing or ask around for word-of-mouth referrals.

To that end, I found it very ironic while writing this book, and surprising, that the television series 60 Minutes aired a segment on "Disability, USA" on October 6, 2013. Wow!

What an affirmation for writing this book and sharing another viewpoint of Social Security Disability Insurance. It was an excellent segment that educated its viewers on the U.S. Disability Fund, and how SSDI is used by American people who are unable to work due to illness or injury.

The CBS 60 Minutes segment initially aired on October 6, 2013, and rebroadcasted on June 29, 2014 mentioned the Federal Disability Program provides service to approximately 12 million people and had a significant budget of over $130+ billion. To compare with other government departmental budgets, it was acknowledged this budget (in 2012) was larger than a combined budget of the Justice Department, Labor Department and the Department of Homeland Security.

The segment also covers the Federal Disability Insurance Program's positives by explaining it is available to assist people financially who have been disabled, and are unable to work. It also covered some disheartening facts such as it being perceived as a secret type of welfare system, coupled with various fraudulent activities, etc.

To put it mildly, the segment also opened up many questions and concerns about the Federal Disability Insurance Program *(Social Security Disability Insurance)* program's representation of claimants by attorneys and/or advocates. For example, it was mentioned in the early 1970's, there were less than 20% of claimants represented by attorneys/advocates, but now, it is perceived as the way to go – get an attorney, kick back, and let them do the work.

My two-cents: *remember attorneys have to be compensated, and the longer the process the better for them, since they will receive payment from the government and also many will receive a percentage of your disability insurance back-pay, etc.* Moving on – it was also mentioned the claimant representation of 20 percent in the 1970's has now increased to over **80%** of representation by attorneys/advocates. What a difference time makes…

This book was written to help potential disability claimants complete the Social Security Disability application process **"on their own"** and to **"keep all of their hard-earned money."** Part Two of this book will clearly explain the **potentiality** of **"how to receive your SSDI benefits within four (4) months."**

As the question in the title of this sub-chapter states, "The Process Decision – "Them or Me?" is where we are in – how **"you"** will plan to apply for Social Security Disability Insurance.

For example, should you hire an attorney and/or advocate; or should you have a family member or caregiver help you with applying; or **can you just do it on your own?** As mentioned in the Prologue, there are many avenues you can take to apply, but, if you can:

1. **Read with understanding,**
2. **Use a computer comfortably,**
3. **Feel comfortable and confident to speak on your own behalf to an SSA representative and,**
4. **Believe you can take control and apply on your own to reap your benefits, then the answer to the sub-chapter title question is "Me!"**

To build confidence in taking your next step with this journey, say to yourself and speak loudly, **"I can do this. I will do it. And, I will complete the SSDI application process and receive my disability award benefits within four (4) months on my own!" YOU** can do it! I did it, and received my disability award benefits within four (4) months

– and so can <u>YOU</u>! Let's proceed immediately, and move forward to the **"TAKE ACTION"** section – **PART TWO!**

PART TWO

WHAT ARE SUCCESS POINTS?

There is no algorithmic method to successfully apply for Social Security Disability Insurance (SSDI) and receive your benefits within a four (4) month period. But, first of all I strongly recommend that to apply you use the Internet. The Internet helps record your entries, keeps you and SSDI simultaneously on track, and is an excellent tool to expedite the application process because it is in real time and data does not get lost in the paper shuffle or on someone's desk. It is well documented and the Internet application will become your best friend while applying for SSDI.

Secondly, it is essential you remember **two Success Points** to **QUICKLY Receive your SSDI** and they are:

Success Point #1 (SP#1): <u>NO FEAR</u> – Do It Now!

Success Point #2 (SP#2): Treat People with <u>RESPECT</u>

You may ask, **"What's so special about Success Points?"** Good question, and there is a good answer for it. But before we continue with the answer, please read the following. ***<u>IMPORTANT NOTE</u>***: if you are interested to learn the more **<u>technical</u> "reasoning and explanation"** of how to receive Social Security Disability Insurance benefits within four (4) months, the answers are located in **<u>Part Two</u>** in the **original "Apply for Disability On-Your-Own" book**. ISBN: 978-0-9863876-0-9. Sold on Amazon, B&N, etc.

Going back to the last paragraph and moving forward – the answer to the aforementioned question of, **"What's so special about Success Points**?" is as follows: both of the **Success Points** greatly influence the end result of the applicant being approved to receive a <u>timely</u> **SSDI Notice of Award** *(i.e., your benefits)*.

The **Success Points** are a focal point *(no pun intended)* of <u>your</u> **mission** to receive <u>your</u> **SSDI benefits** in a timely manner. For example, it is extremely important that follow-up is done with SSDI personnel **IMMEDIATELY** on **every occasion** you are contacted by them. Let's briefly cover each Success Point as follows:

<u>Success Point #1 (SP#1)</u>: <u>NO FEAR</u> – Do It Now!

When you receive documents via any media of communication or telephone calls, always closely read the information and/or take the calls. For the information/data that is distributed to you from SSDI personnel, it is **extremely important** and **imperative** that you closely take time to review it, and **promptly respond back** as noted in the requested information. If you are **NOT** on top of the situation and current, your SSDI application processing **will**

be delayed and you can **forget about** receiving your Notice of Award in a quick time frame.

Therefore – **always heed** to **all** communications and **promptly respond**. For example, medical examinations may be required and you should immediately respond, establish your appointments, and be prepared with all required and requested documents for that medical examination appointment. If you wait and let the documents sit in your mailbox or on the kitchen table, and then you decide a week later to make an appointment, etc. a delay in your SSDI Notice of Award will be evident.

Remember during your application time frame, your **priority** is to **ALWAYS** respond back to The Social Security Administration (SSA) **IMMEDIATELY**. Remember SSA is processing your SSDI application, and time is of the essence. Your life as it relates to **receiving SSDI benefits** in a timely manner is in their hands. Don't be a sloth and question yourself…have **NO FEAR – DO IT NOW!**

Success Point #2 (SP#2): Treat People with <u>RESPECT</u>
The other Success Point is to focus on people, i.e., the SSA staff, doctors, family, etc. It is very important that during this

application process you treat people in a **"positive and respectful"** manner. In life it is important to treat people the way you want to be treated, and that same rule applies here and is necessary to expedite your SSDI application process. This also includes as stated earlier in SP#1 to respond back quickly to SSA personnel, and also build a connection with your SSA contact person.

For example, when an applicant receives a notice or confirmation of receipt, etc. from an SSDI office, the contact person's name and contact information are usually typed in and made available to the applicant. Many times, we'll look at the listed name and file it, or even throw out the document. This person is essential to your application being processed and "their name and who they are" could become "golden" to your SSDI benefits being expeditiously received.

Therefore, it is extremely imperative that you, 1) keep the document close at hand and do not discard it; and 2) build a positive and real relationship with every SSDI contact name that is given to you via mail, email, fax, telephone, etc. For example, if you're talking on the telephone with an SSA representative, engage in a one-minute conversation and ask them how they are doing, etc. Showing "sincere" care and concern to the SSA representative could be helpful to them that day, and possibly yourself.

The key to creating a people connection is to build a "real" relationship with each designated SSDI department contact person who is introduced via email, mail, fax, etc. It is key to always follow-up on each transaction and date/time stamp all communications. How to build a true relationship is to be real and truthful. Always be positive and appreciative of every SSDI contact person. It is extremely important that your relationship building with everyone involved is "true and real." Do not put on an act. People will feel an act, and it's not for this purpose.

Go deep within yourself and make these moments of building relationships real with humility. Positive effects will come from your authenticity. Also, it is important to always project a professional, yet kind manner, when interacting with SSDI staff. For example, when on the telephone, put a smile on your face and always thank them for helping you. A smile does actually penetrate through the telephone. It really does. It can be felt. Try it. This action will help remind the

SSDI staff representative that behind every application is a "human being" needing their help and assistance.

Overall Keys to Success:

- Be professional and positive when interacting with your designated SSDI contacts. This will help you in gathering next step information on what to expect, and how to potentially proceed with your SSDI application.

- Always respond back immediately to communications from the SSA in establishing all areas of processing, such as, document requests, establishing medical examinations, etc. Do not procrastinate at any level of communications.

- It is important to follow-up, document, and let your SSDI contacts know your needs and build a relationship from the beginning to the end result of receiving your SSDI benefits.

- Build a "real" relationship with each designated SSDI department contact person.

- Project a positive image, that is appreciative, professional, confident and yet kind when interacting from all communication vehicles.

ANOTHER IMPORTANT NOTE!

This book was specifically designed and created to give you **"tips"** and **"recommendations"** on how to navigate through the Social Security Disability Insurance process in an expeditious way, and when/how to "project yourself" in order to receive your Disability benefits in a faster manner. With that said, whenever a tip or recommendation is implied, there will be an outlined message to acknowledge on which **"Success Point" (SP#1: <u>NO FEAR</u> – Do It Now! / SP#2: Treat People with <u>RESPECT</u> or both)** is being activated and/or used during your application process.

WHAT TO DO NOW?

There are many stories about how long the SSDI application process takes, who gets paid and when, such as attorneys and advocates being involved, and how to apply. Since I opted to "do it on my own," it was time for me to apply and start the process. Following is how I started my SSDI application, and I'm honored to share my personal experience and give helpful tips as follows:

In order to assist me to remember the date I initially applied on the Internet was very helpful, and that date was acknowledged by the SSA. The date my mother passed away on November 19, was the date I applied and began the application process. At first I was uncomfortable to apply on that date, but I was perusing the SSDI website two days earlier on Nov. 17, and decided to go ahead and apply on November 19th. My reflection of the day I lost my mother was very sad and yet peaceful, because she would no longer suffer on this earth. Five years prior to that date, she had a massive stroke and my Dad cared for her every day. She had lost her left leg, being amputated due to diabetes, paralyzed on left side of her body and for those five years after her stroke, my husband and I commuted from Chicago to Pittsburgh one weekend per month to help Dad take care of Mom, and to check up on him.

It was fulfilling to help, and yet it opened my eyes to watch this very confident, vibrant, prayer warrior, caring, and can-do woman change in front of my eyes to being paralyzed in a wheelchair with difficulty speaking. She was a blessing to many people, and always had an outreach to people less fortunate than us. She was a beautiful and strong lady.

To that end, my Dad was the epitome of a wonderful husband, who always said he was committed in taking his marriage vows seriously and to heart, and that he would take care of my Mom and he did. Words cannot express my love and appreciation for my own wonderful husband, Tony, who traveled with me to help my parents during that timeframe, and we have been happily married since 1989, best friends forever and he has been my caregiver. . . I love you, Tony.

Beautiful memories of my Mommy helped me with the process to apply for my SSDI benefits on her day of no more suffering on this earth. Also, applying on that date helped my memory when communicating with SSDI personnel.

SP#1: NO FEAR – Do It Now! For example, when an SSDI representative would look up my records and request the date I started my Internet application, I knew immediately it was November 19th with a smile of gratitude. **Recommendation:** initially apply via the Internet on a special memorable date, that will give you a reflection of good memories, hope and confidence. I did, and four months later received my SSDI Notice of Award. I also recommend using children's birthdates, anniversary dates, etc. something positive and memorable that will help give you confidence and a "can-do" manner of broaching the SSDI application process.

Start Your Application Process

As mentioned in our last chapter's first paragraph, **"What Are Success Points?"** it is highly recommended from experience, to use the Internet to apply for your Social Security Disability Insurance (SSDI) benefits. Per the SSA, located on their **"Checklist – Adult Disability Interview"** (see Starter Kit below), is the following first statement, *"We encourage you to begin the application process online."* It is highly recommended that you read the **Social Security Disability Adult Starter Kit** information, which is located on their website at www.socialsecurity.gov or www.ssa.gov and **search** for Adult Disability Starter Kit.

The Disability Starter Kit has a checklist that gives you information to prepare for your application processing in general – either via online *(preferred method)*, telephone interview or in person at your local Social Security office.

The Disability Starter Kit also helps in your preparedness to: 1.) ensure you meet the requirements to apply online, and 2.) collect the data required to complete the Disability application process for SSDI. As stated, the SSDI Internet online application program – records and saves your entries, and is an excellent real time tool. So, let's not delay and start your application process now!

Here we go:

Step 1:

- Go online to: www.socialsecurity.gov
  or www.ssa.gov
- Click on "Apply for Disability"
- And, that's it!

The "Apply for Disability" webpage is rich with information, and should make you feel comfortable with the start of your application process. Since I applied, the SSDI office has been continuously enhancing their website and program information, therefore, I highly recommend you review this webpage closely, and also click to "review and print-out" the pdf's listed under Publications.

As of September 2016, the .pdf Publications noted on the webpage are: 1) Disability Benefits, and 2). Other Disability Publications. In summary, the "Disability Benefits" publication covers many aspects of the SSDI program, such as: who can receive Social Security Disability benefits, how to apply, when to apply, family benefits, Medicare, etc. and is very informational summarizing the overall Social Security Disability Insurance program.

Again, The Social Security Administration has done an excellent job in keeping the SSDI Internet application data updated, and has made exceptional enhancements since I applied back in 2012. Kudos to The Social Security Administration and the SSDI office!

If your comfort level is mediocre in using the Internet, there are two other methods to use in applying for SSDI and those are:

1.) Call Social Security at 1.800.772.1213 to set-up an appointment to meet with your **local Social Security Office** to personally file a disability claim, **or**

2.) **Call** the aforementioned telephone number and request to make a telephone appointment, and have a representative take your disability claim over the telephone.

SP#2: Treat People with RESPECT As previously mentioned, the Internet is the preferred method to expedite your claim and can be more easily recorded and tracked. But, if you need to file via telephone or local office appointment, it is highly recommended to closely review the aforementioned Adult Disability Starter Kit's section: **"Checklist – Adult Disability Interview"** which goes into detail by giving a checklist for the disability benefits eligibility interview **via telephone or in the local office.**

Always remember to be **"Prepared, Professional and Polite"** to whomever you speak and meet with – and those **3 P's** will be on your side to help your SSDI process be moved closer and closer for you to receive your SSDI Notice of Award in a short period of time.

DISABILITY BENEFIT APPLICATION

We will start with the first section of the application process which is the **Disability Benefit Application** or (Application for Benefits).

When applying online, the day you register and set-up your online account is the date the SSA will use as your "official registration date" for the application. As mentioned, my date was November 19, 2012. Wow! It was official! You are given six (6) months to complete the application (with your e-signature) or "you may lose Social Security benefits."

Per the SSA, "If this date falls on the weekend or is a Federal holiday, we (they) must receive the signed application by the following business day." So, to keep this real, as mentioned – I initially applied on 11/19/2012 and officially completed my first section of the "application" on 11/29/2012. (**PLEASE NOTE:** this completion was for the "first" section only, and was **not** for the entire application being completed.) How did this 10-day process happen? Here's the answer: SSA gives an **Application Number** *(a re-entry number)* that is active for the entire application process, from the first initial date of Internet entry into your application to receiving your decision being made on your SSDI application.

ANOTHER NOTE: the "Application Number" *(a re-entry number)* they give you is a **keeper. DO NOT** discard or misplace this number, and definitely **DO NOT** share it with anyone. This provides total access into your SSDI application. This **Application Number** *(a re-entry number)* stays with you during the entire application process, even during the "waiting period," and it is the access pathway in checking your SSDI Application Status, i.e., by entering this Application Number *(a re-entry number)* along with your Social Security Number.

To answer the aforementioned "10-day question" – here is the answer: during that ten (10) day timeframe, I was able to update my application when able, and always had to use my Application Number *(a re-entry number)* ...in order to regain access into my SSDI application. It was great! All you have to do is:

1.) Type in the following webpage: https://secure.ssa.gov/iClaim/dib
2.) Click "Return to Saved Application Process"
3.) Next, type in your "Re-Entry Number" and Social Security Number then, click enter.

The system will take you directly back to your last entry on the application. That's it!

VERY IMPORTANT NOTE: SSA advises the following, **"If you lose or forget your Application Number *(a re-entry number)*, you will have to begin this application over again and you will lose all the information you already entered."** To that end, always remember the Application Number *(a re-entry number)* is a keeper and to – **keep it close**. Also, if for some reason you are not able to return back to your Internet application, and still want to apply for SSDI via another method, just call the Social

Security telephone number at 1.800.772.1213, and they will have representatives available to assist you.

Now back to personal sharing: please know the evening of November 29, 2012 was a "happy and fulfilling" night for me! Yay! I officially received an online confirmation from the SSA that my "first" section of the claim application was completed and received on November 29, 2012 at 9:33:21PM. Amazing! Also, the online confirmation gave information for next steps which was to complete my online Adult Disability Report (SSA-3368) and medical release form, "Authorization to Disclose Information to the Social Security Administration (SSA-827). Let's first briefly cover the medical release form.

The SSA developed an online medical Authorization Form for applicants to review and e-sign. The online medical release form is automatically filled-in with your personal information and it only requires a "click" to accept. In summary, it takes all of one minute to review and e-sign your medical release Authorization Form, and then it is done.

SP#1: NO FEAR – Do It Now! Now, there are options to print and mail the Authorization Form to your local Social

Security office, but, that does compromise speed in receiving your SSDI benefit claim processed expeditiously. Friendly reminder – time is of the essence, and taking time to either mail or visit the local office could potentially compromise a couple of days in processing and receiving your SSDI benefits. It is **strongly recommended** to process the medical release Authorization Form **online and use your e-signature**. Remember to always "print and file" this form and all documents during your application process.

SSDI RECEIPT LETTER AND CONFIRMATIONS

After you receive an online confirmation of your application being completed, a hard copy letter of acknowledgement and additional information will arrive to your mailing address from the Social Security Administration's Disability Insurance (SSDI).

SP#1: NO FEAR – Do It Now! This letter will again confirm receipt of your Disability Benefit Application, and explain if additional information is needed in order to complete your total application, as it relates to directing you to complete the Disability Report online. Also, the letter will give your local Social Security Office address, telephone number and your Representative's name with their telephone number and extension.

SP#1: NO FEAR – Do It Now! and SP#2: Treat People with RESPECT Now is your time to take **immediate action!** Once you receive the hard copy letter with a request for additional proof of income and your local contact person information, it is now time to contact that person, in order to help expedite the request for additional data. (i.e., proof of income, etc.)

[RULE #1: Contact your local Social Security Administration contact representative immediately, once you receive their information to start building your "one-on-one" relationship.] If your SSA representative is not available and your call goes to voicemail, leave a message with your name, telephone number, and claim number. Also, leave a brief message and explain the purpose of your call. Your telephone call purpose is to introduce yourself, and to request a brief discussion of how to send your proof of income to that person or office in an expeditious and approved mode of communication.

Since we're keeping this real, I did have to call numerous times and left voicemail messages. After leaving the voicemail messages, I was happy to receive a call-back, and that call was golden. Yay! My SSA representative was apologetic of the call-back delay and also empathetic to my calls. That person wanted to help expedite my claim, and versus having me mail in the documents requested, they gave me the "FAX" number to send the proof of income via fax. The SSA representative also wanted to stay connected, and that started the building of an "on-going" relationship.

SP#1: NO FEAR – Do It Now! and SP#2: Treat People with RESPECT

[RULE #2: Always find out what FAX number can be used to expedite your application processing.] My SSA representative gave me their fax number and this significantly reduced turnaround time of overall "snail mail" (mailing via U.S. Postal Service and SSA in-house mail processing). No matter on what occasion – when information is requested and for it to be mailed in – ask the SSA representative this following question, "How can we expedite the process, and can I use your fax number to send the documents?" Every time (100%) an incident occurred and I would ask this question to "fax versus mail" – every time – the SSA representative would say "yes" and they gave me their fax number to send what was requested.

REMEMBER -- Always ask for your SSA representative's <u>fax number</u>. The fax request will activate **Success Point #1: NO FEAR – Do It Now! and build on Success Point #2: Treat People with RESPECT** quickly. For example, one time I faxed over 20 pages in one incident, and the turnaround time was phenomenal for the request. Think about it. From the time it takes you to compile the information and place it in an envelope – mail it – have it received and placed through in-house mail to be stamped – sent from the mail room to the SSA representative and then placed in their "inbox" could be days. **SP#1: NO FEAR – Do It Now! and SP#2: Treat People with RESPECT**

Again, one more time – ask for the **FAX number and <u>fax it.</u> VISUALIZE: within 5 minutes** the information is sent and received. Also, always keep and print-out your fax transmittal receipt page to ensure confirmation from an electronic viewpoint. And then, call the SSA representative back to verify with them, that you sent the fax and request their confirmation that – they are in receipt of the fax.

Okay. Stay with me. We have covered: confirmation of first section of application being completed, hard copy received of confirmation and additional documents needed, medical release form, and fax versus mail, which are **extremely IMPORTANT** to manage in order to expedite your application.

In closing of this segment, the first section of your application, **"Disability Benefit Application"** is completed. We will now segue to another section of the process and that is the, **"Adult Disability Report (ADR)."**

ADULT DISABILITY REPORT

As aforementioned – let's get back on track with the application process, and move into the **ADR**. Now you should go and sign back into your Internet online application, and start on the **Adult Disability Report (ADR)**. As mentioned, this report is separate, and as of my application process, it even has its **"own" re-entry number** to sign-on/off and return later in order to complete the report.

The Adult Disability Report requests and covers more details of explaining your illness, such as list of doctors, medications taken, prescribing doctors, medical tests, employment, education, and insurance/worker's compensation claims. Therefore, it may take time to complete the report in order to ensure accuracy of your claim. It is highly recommended to be rested and complete the report in a couple of Internet sessions, by using your Re-entry Number.

[RULE #3: Take your time to complete your entire application, especially the Adult Disability Report section. It is imperative you ensure accuracy and triple check your data.] Ensuring accuracy will avoid potential issues, which in turn could alleviate rejection of your SSDI claim. I strongly recommend you use your option to re-enter the Adult Disability Report by using your Social Security Number and Re-entry Number. The website will explain how to sign-off, but, always remember to click the "Sign Off (finish later)" option. SSDI will save your data, and when you are fresh and ready, you can proceed back to the report:

1.) Go to the website:

www.socialsecurity.gov/adultdisabilityreport

2.) Click the "Return to Saved Application Process"

3.) As noted, type in your Re-entry Number and Social Security Number

As a tip – keep the Re-entry Number close at hand and **DO NOT** share it with anyone. On a great note – with your Re-entry Number there are no limitations on the number of times you can access the Adult Disability Report system. Awesome!

Per the SSA, **"IF YOU LOSE YOUR RE-ENTRY NUMBER BEFORE YOU SUBMIT THE REPORT, YOU WILL NOT BE ABLE TO GO BACK TO THIS REPORT AND FINISH."** You would have to begin a brand new Adult Disability Report and would receive a new Re-entry Number. Per the SSA, no one can help you regain access without your Re-entry Number and, "all of the information you previously entered will be lost." In summary, **protect** your Adult Disability Report: **Re-entry Number**. Ensure you do all you can to **not lose or discard** your Re-entry Number.

As promised, we are keeping this book real and succinct for your reading and learning purposes. As a friendly review, from 11/29/2012 to 12/10/2012 I worked on the Adult Disability Report (ADR) updating it numerous times and triple checking it for accuracy. After much thought and getting to the point of your mission, I will not cover the entire Adult Disability Report (ADR) but, feel compelled to bring one very special section of it to your attention when completing the report SP#2: **Treat People with RESPECT**.

One area on the ADR that is extremely imperative to **complete in detail** with passionate and clear thoughts is the last section, called **"Remarks."** This is your way to **respectfully** express what you have been going through, your needs, and asking for approval of your benefit claim. It is your expression to the reader to understand your disability and how it has impacted your life in the past, present, and future. To leave this section blank, or to just doodle a note or two is not acceptable as being a **Success Point** in expediting your SSDI application.

Once again -- **REPEAT,** SP#2: **Treat People with RESPECT** is activated in the **"Remarks"** section. This section is the time to **respectfully** tell **your story**, express **your passion**, request **your need** for a benefit claim approval, and last but not least, **build a relationship** with the staff person reading/reviewing your records. Do not be ashamed to state your case and tell your story to the reader. I hope my duplication of explaining the "Remarks" section

– has expressed its sincere importance, and that it should be written in an explanatory, passionate manner – in order to explain and **ask for approval** and to also **expedite** your claim benefits, so that you can **focus on healing** and **regain a new, solid purpose in your life** towards **moving on**.

While working on the Adult Disability Report (ADR) during that timeframe, I had no interaction with SSA staff only the Internet application and staying focused towards getting the ADR completed and submitted. The day is now December 10, 2012 at 7:16:29 p.m. Eastern time, and my ADR was just completed via online. Yay! I received a "Receipt for Your Records" confirmed notification that my "Online Adult Disability Report and electronically signed and dated Medical Release Form" were received. Another Yay! It is done!

CONNECTION WITH LOCAL SOCIAL SECURITY OFFICE

From the point of the online "Receipt for Your Records" notification confirming your Entire Claim Application – the application process is then moved towards being administered by your local Social Security Office, and next steps are advised.

Per the SSA, "It takes about 120 days to make a disability decision. Every case is different. We may take more or less time on your case." Wow. The notification also addressed more information may be needed, such as the potential of more medical evidence being required – where the SSA may request the claimant to visit one of their doctors at no charge.

Additionally, the "Receipt of Your Records" gives next steps, i.e., contact information for the local Social Security Office, etc. This receipt is very informative and is a "keeper."

[RULE #4: Keep all receipts and confirmation notices received by SSA close at hand, and do not share with anyone unless that person is assisting with your application, and needs to process your personal identification data and disability information.]

Moving on in real person application time – the date and time is now December 27, 2012 at 3:19 p.m. Pacific time and a form letter from the local SSA office was generated to send an "Application Summary for Disability Insurance Benefits Confirmation Number" letter, titled "Checking the Status of Your Claim," along with instructions on how to access your claim status. The document indicates a small waiting time period (approximately 5 days) before being able to check claim status, and it gives the SSA webpage for claim access.

SP#1: NO FEAR – Do It Now!

The letter also noted a confirmation number for the claim and to remember to guard this number carefully. As noted, this is the "Confirmation Number" that is key to your entire application. The SSA advises to not store this number with other personal information and to not give it to anyone. Most important: it is also noted, "Social Security employees will NEVER ask for your Confirmation Number." And, not to scare you – but the following is noted in the letter, "…disability claims take longer to process than other types of Social Security claims because we need to obtain sufficient medical evidence to show that you are disabled."

As mentioned – please do not get scared, so now is the time for you to acquire patience, meditation, perseverance, and reflect on how great it is to have this opportunity and look forward to the future. Approximately a month will pass by, and it will be a quiet month of patience and probably an excellent time to read a good book. Remember, the process is occurring and no news is good news for this time period!

Medical Examinations and other Documentation

So…to continue sharing my journey in real time – from December 27, 2012 to the first of February 2013 was a quiet time period, which was to be expected. My doctors and the hospital staff were very accommodating and quick to respond to the SSA medical record requests. Many thanks to my doctors, their staff and hospital staff. But, we know patience is a virtue and it was now February. So, when Monday February 4th came around there was some anxiety on my part to find out next steps. I calmed down and reminded myself that Mondays are usually not good days to resolve issues or ask questions in a business customer service environment.

Therefore, I waited until Tuesday, February 5, 2013 at 1:51 p.m. *(after lunch time)* and activated **SP1 and SP2**, and then called the local Social Security Office. It was Tuesday, and they happily advised me of next steps for my application, and that it was now in another department and division. The Department of Social Services was the new department, and the "Division of Disability Determinations (DDS)" was under that department. The SSA representative offered to transfer my call to the DDS analyst scheduler to find out the status of my claim. SP#1: NO FEAR – Do It Now!

HELPFUL TIP: whenever you're on **any** business call and the person **"offers to transfer your call,"** always **remember to request that actual telephone "number" before the call is transferred** – in the event the call is not transferred with success. This new Division was a critical point in the application process, and the need to expedite with "no call transfer issues" was of the utmost importance and urgency. Therefore, I **"immediately"** requested the Division's telephone number just in case the call transfer did not work. Fortunately, the call transfer was successful. But, if it was not, I would have had to start back and call the local Social Security office for information, and start the new division contact process over again.

When the DDS analyst scheduler answered the call, I put on my "professional, polite face" and spoke with the analyst scheduler and immediately began building a relationship. At that time, it was discussed there was unfortunately, **no one** scheduled on my claim. "Ugh." After we discussed the situation and more relationship building, by the end of the call, a **"Disability Evaluation Analyst (DEA)"** was scheduled for my claim. **"Yay!"** I was advised by the analyst scheduler to expect to hear from the Disability Evaluation Analyst (DEA) **soon**.

ANOTHER HELPFUL TIP: if you have the opportunity to speak with a DEA scheduler and they know who will be selected as your DEA, always remember <u>before</u> hanging up the telephone "to ask" for your DEA's name and contact information, such as their telephone number. This will help ensure you will be able to speak/connect with your DEA sooner versus later. Remember, those **3P's always be "Prepared, Professional and Polite."** SP#1: NO FEAR – Do It Now! and SP#2: Treat People with RESPECT

Back to real time. In a few days, I received an envelope from my DEA via Postal mail with enclosed documents dated, February 6, 2013. "Wow." Well, February 2013 came with much sunshine of activity and hope, with requested documentation and medical exam(s). February and March were very active months and many **"Success Points"** were activated. <u>**Quick question:**</u> **what if I had never called on February 5th to activate the Success Points?** <u>**Answer:**</u> Found out from a SSA source that normal processing takes approximately 2-3 weeks for a DEA to be scheduled. **Success Points in Action!** Let's keep moving.

As mentioned, in February medical request forms were sent to me via Postal mail pertaining to verification of my type of illness and disability. I reviewed the package and noticed the following: cover page, fill-in forms, and a return envelope. "Excellent!" It's now time to activate SP1 and SP2! The forms displayed my Disability Evaluation Analyst's (DEA's) name and my Case Number (a new number). Unfortunately, there was no contact number information for the DEA, so, it's time for **SP2!** I recommend that you contact your local Social Security Administration office contact person and ask them for your DEA contact information. That is what I did – and it worked! SP#2: Treat People with RESPECT

When you secure your DEA telephone number, then call that person and introduce yourself and ask them if they can help you expedite your medical forms, additional reports and -- **what you can do to help them make it easier to process your application.** And, always remember to ask for their direct telephone number and fax number. The DEA position is very busy and therefore, do not expect to have lengthy conversations with them. Therefore, when communicating with your DEA, be prepared to ask a quick question and also expect a "quick" answer.

[RULE #5: Always be respectful of your Social Security Administration contacts. They are extremely busy and do not have time for long discussions or additional stress.] When your process is completed, I recommend you write them a letter or note of thanks for their hard work efforts and in helping you.

The medical exams requested were pertinent to my disability. I had to engage in two (2) medical examinations. The exam process was very structured and customer focused. The exam cost is covered by the SSA. The exams are for evaluation only, and not for treatment. Post cards and reminders with a map were mailed out prior to the exam, along with scheduled date, time and address of examination and a telephone number for questions.

Prior to the medical exams, I had to complete reports requesting information on my illness, such as descriptions, daily activities, personal care, ability to get around, social activities, hobbies and interests, etc. and an open page for **"REMARKS."** | SP#2: Treat People with RESPECT |

Friendly reminder: when a **"REMARKS"** section is available on any report – always remember to state your case with the **3P's** and **double check for accuracy**.

The medical examination reports are sent to your home via Postal mail. As mentioned, the reports cover the type of medical appointment, date, time, location and is sent from your DEA. There will also be forms to complete and return back to your DEA via Postal mail with an enclosed return envelope to a PO Box in another city. **SP1 ALERT!!** Whenever a return envelope is enclosed, look on the cover page of the documents to **locate a <u>fax number</u>**.

The majority of data requested from your DEA will have an enclosed return envelope and a cover sheet that will include a "fax number" option that gives you the opportunity to fax your information. Please note, this fax number is not your DEA's direct fax line. It is a fax number that scans your fax and sends your data to your DEA. Again, this step is very imperative to use, as it **removes approximately one week** of **delayed time** in using Postal mail, versus **<u>faxing</u> within one minute.** Also, it is important to closely follow the instructions on these medical examination forms, and remember to triple check for accuracy.

As mentioned, the SSA works with the Department of Social Services within their Disability Determination Service Division (DDSD) in order to complete the claim for medical development and additional evaluation. There are various forms this division generates to claimants. The DEA will send these forms to you and the documents are to be completed. These reports are requested to be returned back to your DEA via Postal mail. SP1 ALERT!!

But, **once again there is a fax number located** on the cover page and for efficiency, I strongly recommend to **fax** the forms back to your DEA. Also, be consistent and accurate in completing the form and do not leave answers blank. Also, just as important as ALL reports, use the **"REMARKS" section** to explain items that may need clarification to the DEA reader.

Decision Made, Sign-Off, Quality Review

First of all – give KUDOS to yourself, the SSA, DDSD, and to the entire process of SSDI. It is almost done – Yay!

So…let's get back to my sharing of this journey's timeline. The medical exams have been completed, all medical records have been received, and now it is "Decision Making" time. I just had my last SSDI medical exam, all documentation was faxed and the date is March 16, 2013. Whew.

Now was the time to go online and check the status of my application. On March 18, 2013 I went online, and it was stated that a decision was still in the process. I did expect to see that notice, since it was only two (2) days since all of my documentation and last medical exam were completed. Then, March 20th came and I decided to log in and check my status again. I thought maybe in another two days, I would see something to make my day – and I did!!

On March 20, 2013, my status report information read as follows: "A decision has been made on your claim. You will receive the official notice of any decision made on your claim by U.S. mail." Then, the last paragraph showed this: "If you need more information you may call us toll-free at ..." $\boxed{\text{SP1}}$ $\boxed{\text{and SP2 ALERT!!}}$ **Success Points ready for takeoff** and action! I immediately called the toll-free number to find out next steps.

The SSA representative was very kind and we chatted for a couple of minutes and she confirmed a decision had been made on my claim. I did ask the result, and was told the next step would be a Quality Review to ensure all items were verified and confirmed. I was told the Quality Review would take approximately 60 days from that date, and I should receive my decision answer by May 19, 2013. "OH NO!!!"

We cannot have another waiting period, but can we? So, **SP2** went into action and the relationship of asking by using the 3P's was covered: what are the next steps, explain the process, etc. And, we also discussed what could be done to expedite the process. She recommended for me to call back to my local Social Security office in five (5) business days. From that point I said, "Thank you. I will wait five (5) business days, and call my local Social Security office contact person." Basically, I repeated what she said to ensure I was listening.

Wow! So close, but, yet so far. Sixty (60) more days of waiting for the Quality Review. Ugh. But, I had faith, and felt it all would result in my favor. I just felt it, prayed and believed.

The Notice of Award

After waiting five (5) business days, I decided to put SP1 and SP2 into action and called my local Social Security contact. Unfortunately, they were not available so I had to leave a voicemail. But, my voicemail was **SP2** into action. For your information, here is a summary of the voicemail. As requested, I gave my name, claim number and then reminded my local SSA contact who I was, and that we had our first connection via telephone back in December, and it had been awhile since we last interacted. Then, I started the reason for my call with excitement, and used the 3P's to the maximum!

For example, reminding my local SSA contact of our previous conversations; giving thanks for their support; and how important they are to me and all the disability claimants needing their help, etc. My local SSA contact person called me back within 24 hours and verbally gave me the good news, that my claim was approved and that I should receive my Notice of Award in a few days! The Quality Review was expedited and all was approved!! The local SSA contact person was happy for me, and I requested them to "please" fax me a copy of the Notice of Award. Surprisingly, the

Notice of Award was immediately faxed to me on March 28, 2013 at 10:37 a.m. Yay!

Let's quickly review the success of SP1 and SP2 being combined and activated:

1.) The Quality Review of six (6) weeks was expedited.

2.) Regular processing would have taken **The Notice of Award** to arrive in my hands via Postal mail in a **few days versus an immediate fax!** For example, the original Award was sent and received via Postal mail, but **the fax** of the **Notice of Award** was immediate verification to confirm **The Notice of Award was approved.**

3.) With combining SP#1: NO FEAR – Do It Now! and SP#2: Treat People with RESPECT by building "real" relationships, it helped expedite the process to have The Notice of Award in my hand immediately, and it brought much peace, hope, and comfort to our home.

Since I applied for **Disability On-My-Own**, the back payments were paid to me in full **(no attorney or advocate fees)**, and monthly disability payments started the following month.

In closing of this process, my personal checklist of completion is as follows:

- Online application completed December 10, 2012.

- The Notice of Award faxed and in hand March 28, 2013. The same faxed document hard copy letter, was dated and mailed via Postal Service on March 31, 2013. **SP1 and SP2** in action to the end-result.

- **Mission Accomplished. Praise the Lord!**

THE BEGINNING OF A "NEW LIFE" CHAPTER

What a journey we had with the writing of this book. I truly hope these words, instructions, and the Success Points will help your online process to receive – your hard-earned **Social Security Disability Insurance (SSDI) "on-your-own"** – is very **successful the first time!**

The key to starting your "New Life Chapter" is to realize your life has changed. You are now classified as disabled on Social Security Disability Insurance, and unable to work. Some of you will regain strength, be restored health-wise, and in a couple or few years may be able to go back to work, or volunteer to help others in need. That would be wonderful!

Thank God, as of this writing I am still in my *"New Life Chapter"* of restoration and recovery. It's amazing how our physical bodies are created to heal after surgeries, injuries, illness, etc. **God is so good!** I am so thankful for living, and to share my experience to sincerely help others with the SSDI process and the **Success Points** with all of you.

I am not the same young, super-energized J.D. that I was known for being, but, I continue to have a vision, mission, strong faith, perseverance, and a drive to share and to sincerely help others. I am still in a recovery mode, but, it is important this **updated Concise Guide book** comes out to support the first publication in order to help SSDI applicants who want to **apply on their own** without attorney/advocate assistance. Remember, if you are of sound mind and can manage the following:

1.) Read with understanding.

2.) Use a computer comfortably.

3.) Feel comfortable and confident to speak on your own behalf to an SSA representative and,

4.) Believe you can take control, then **<u>APPLY ON-YOUR-OWN</u>** and reap all of your benefits!

In closing, live life the way you want to live it, and remember to activate the **Success Points** to get what you desire in the essence of life. **Godspeed, and much success to you!**

FIVE "CAN-DO" RULES TO REMEMBER

RULE #1: Contact your local Social Security Administration (SSA) representative **immediately**, once you receive their contact information to start **building your "one-on-one" relationship.**

RULE #2: Always find out what FAX number can be used to **expedite your application** processing.

RULE #3: Take time to **complete** your **ENTIRE application.** It is imperative you **ensure accuracy** and **triple check** your data on all areas of your application.

RULE #4: Keep ALL receipts and confirmation notices received by SSA close at hand, and **do not share** your re-entry number(s) with anyone, unless that person is assisting with your application and needs to process your personal identification data and disability information.

RULE #5: Always be respectful of your Social Security Administration contact person(s) time, role, and responsibility. They are extremely busy, and **do not have time** for long discussions, disagreements, or additional stress. Remember to **build** your relationships **respectfully, and with professionalism and kindness.**

THE ROAD MAP TO: "YOU CAN DO THIS!"

As noted, this book has two parts – Part One is to assist with help in stabilizing your emotional state, and to focus on being positive and adjusting to a new season of change. Part Two of the book covers "how to" apply for Social Security Disability Insurance with personal examples to assist in understanding the online disability application process.

While writing, I felt it would be helpful to have a solid and easy **"Road Map"** in "how to" do this application process, and named it, **"You Can Do This!"** As mentioned, I did it "on-my-own" and so can you! Remember in the beginning of Part Two, the first chapter **"What are Success Points?"** covers the success points of focus which are: **Success Points (SP #1): NO FEAR – Do It Now!** and **(SP#2): Treat People with RESPECT**. These **Success Points** are very helpful in navigating through the overall disability application process.

To make it an easier process, following is a road map of the expedited steps, and what to look for while completing your application with reference to the **Success Points**. Please remember to read **ALL** of your **SSDI application** information, and do **NOT** only use this checklist to complete your disability application.

At the time of the printing of this book, Social Security Disability Insurance application updates and changes may have occurred, and are **ALWAYS** being conducted via the Internet, therefore as mentioned – **PLEASE DO NOT** only use this Road Map checklist to complete your disability application.

Also, it is imperative you **do not give a quick glance over the SSDI actual application** and **information requested**, but use this as a book of information **ONLY** as *"reference tips"* to assist in ways **to expedite your disability application process.**

The ROAD MAP: "You Can Do This!!"

NOTE: Each SSA Disability Insurance applicant and case is different. Also, the Road Map tips may vary in sequence or actual procedure due to the ever-changing SSDI process. The following is an example of what may occur, as it did from personal experience. The following **does not guarantee** the exact process will occur in the same format, but, the **"Success Points and 3P's- Prepared, Professional and Polite"** are <u>solid recommendations</u> that will significantly assist you with this process – **and also <u>with life</u> in general as it relates to dealing with consumer (you) to business relationships.** For example: having an issue to resolve with a business colleague, store manager, airlines, store, etc. When you have completed each of the following numbered **"Road Map"** tips, check the square box to the left of the number to ensure completion of that tactic. See following checked example when completed: ☑

☐ 1.) Once you find out that you have a disabling illness, and it is confirmed for a significant period of time, immediately sign-up and register on the **Internet** for your Social Security Disability Insurance (SSDI) application benefit claim. Go to the website: <u>www.socialsecurity.gov</u> or <u>www.ssa.gov</u>

☐ 2.) Search for – and review the Social Security Starter Disability Kit to ensure you qualify to apply online. If so, move forward! **SP#1: NO FEAR – Do It Now!**

☐ 3.) Complete first section of SSDI application process, which is called the, "Disability Benefit Application." SP#1: NO FEAR – Do It Now!

☐ 4.) Once completed, you will receive confirmation of the Disability Benefit Application being completed via an online notification.

☐ 5.) Next, you will receive a hard copy letter in the mail stating next steps, and to complete the second section of the online SSDI application process which is called the, Adult Disability Report. SP#1: NO FEAR – Do It Now!

☐ 6.) If SSA makes a request for you to send additional documents, contact your SSA representative via telephone, and request they give you their fax number to expedite sending versus sending it through U.S. Postal Service (USPS) mail. SP#1: NO FEAR – Do It Now! / SP#2: Treat People with RESPECT

☐ 7.) The Adult Disability Report (ADR) covers reporting the details to explain your illness, and is a very important document that "states your case." Read the ADR closely, follow the details, and triple check your work. SP#1: NO FEAR – Do It Now!

☐ 8.) The ADR has a "REMARKS" section at the end of the application. It is imperative you use this section to tell your story, express your passion and request your need.

SP#1: NO FEAR – Do It Now! / SP#2: Treat People with RESPECT

☐ 9.) The online Medical Release form will need to be completed at this time. Recommend to continue online and use e-signature to approve the form, if you concur. Then, you are done. SP#1: NO FEAR – Do It Now!

☐ 10.)Once you have completed your ADR and electronically signed and dated your Medical Release Form you will receive a confirmation.

☐ 11.)Plan to receive a form letter from your local SSA office acknowledging receipt of your application, and informing you how to check the Status of your Claim. SP#1: NO FEAR – Do It Now!

☐ 12.) There is a waiting period where medical information has been requested from your doctors, hospitals, etc. and being reviewed. Also, your claim will now be moved and worked in another department and division to schedule medical examinations, etc. Additionally, a new team will handle your claim, for evaluation called, Disability Evaluation Analysts (DEA). This team is under the Department of Social Services, and is in the Division of Disability Determinations (DDS).

SP1 and SP2 MAXIMIZED!

☐ 13.) Many Success Points occur during the above #12's process, and it is highly recommended to closely read the section, "Medical Examinations and Other Documentations" to completely understand how to manage through the process expeditiously without an issue. **SP1 and SP2 ALERT!!**

☐ 14.) A Decision will be made, and there will be a Sign-Off and Quality Review process. The timing varies in each of these areas and the key will be to stay focused on patience, people interaction and diligent follow-up using the 3P's – being "Prepared,

Professional and Polite." SP#2: Treat People with
RESPECT

☐ 15.) If all of the aforementioned is completed with **favor** of your claim, you will receive **"The Notice of Award"** for your Social Security Disability Insurance claim.

Congratulations!!!

You successfully did it, and
Applied for Disability "On-Your-Own!"

REFERENCES AND RESOURCES

CBS 60 Minutes Overtime. *"Disability, USA"* aired October 6, 2013, Rebroadcast on June 29, 2014. www.cbsnews.com/news/disability-usa-2

The American Heritage Dictionary of the English Language, Fourth Edition. (2000) Boston, MA: Houghton Mifflin Company.

The Holy Bible, New King James Version. (1988) Nashville, TN: Thomas Nelson Publishers.

U.S. The Social Security Administration's Website. http://www.socialsecurity.gov and/or www.ssa.gov November 2012 to September 2016.

Made in the USA
Middletown, DE
25 October 2022